TAKING CARE OF YOUR TEMPLE

TEMPLE CARETAKERS MANUAL

JULIE A. WARD-WEATHINGTON, BSN RN

Warning! Please read this first.

The purpose of this manual is to provide information and education about health. The author and publisher do not directly or indirectly dispense medical advice or prescribe the use of fasting or diet as a form of treatment for sickness without medical approval. Nutritionists and other experts in the field of health and nutrition hold widely varying views. Again, the author and publisher do not intend to diagnose or prescribe. The author and publisher intend to offer health information to help you cooperate with your doctor or other health practitioners in your mutual quest for health. In the event you use this information without your doctor's or health practitioner's approval, you prescribe for yourself. This remains your constitutional right. The author and publisher assume no responsibility.

Table of Contents

Table of Contents (cont'd)

Foreword

A healthy balanced lifestyle is something everyone should desire to achieve and maintain, but this is not always the case. Have you ever seen a brother or sister in Christ with a great anointing, but you feared for them because they were overweight, stressed and made poor lifestyle choices? You could see the result of their choices adversely affecting them. Or perhaps YOU are that person. Please know that it is God's will and desire for ALL of his people to have balance and to be healthy both spiritually and naturally.

The Temple Care Takers manual provides realistic changes you can easily make to transition into the healthy, vibrant person God intended you to be. It is unique because it's designed to address the total man-spirit, soul and body. You will find a wealth of information on how to stop making bad choices and start developing good habits. You will no longer spend money on fad diets that provide a temporary quick solution. You will learn options that can be realistically maintained. It's the Father's will for you to be blessed and whole! You will know exactly what God's desire is for you by learning what the scriptures say about YOU, God's beloved.

The vision for Temple Care Takers was given to Julie Ward-Weathington many years ago. God showed her His heart's desire for His people to walk in total health in every aspect of their lives. This manual is the result of that impartation. She is a registered nurse by profession, and has an Alternative Health and Wellness Certification with an extensive background in mental health. But more importantly, she is a visionary that God has blessed with Kingdom insight to help build His end-time army. By applying the principles contained in this manual, men and women of God will be able to walk in the spirit AND be healthy vessels, advancing God's Kingdom agenda.

Margaret Thames

Testimonials

"I would like to thank Apostle Julie and Father God for the Vision of Temple Care Taker Classes. Total health care is vital to wholeness in Mind, Body, & Soul; and renewing the mind through applied principles of God's Word. For example, forgiveness releases you to be healed in your soul; and then healing your emotions helps your body to open up to be physically healed as well. I know because in doing the class and assignments, many areas in my life have been renewed and restored and healed." -**Eva**

"Constantly condemning myself, feeling guilty when I say "no" and worrying about what others may say, putting everyone and everything before my spiritual and physical needs, and not recognizing the depth of God's love for me was how I was before taking TCT classes and being delivered. I recommend TCT classes for anyone who is truly ready to change their life." -**Annetta**

"I was impressed, inspired and informed by Temple Care Takers. Now I am healed. I was overweight, had high blood pressure, and type 2 diabetes with borderline high cholesterol. Now I am no longer a diabetic with high blood pressure. My cholesterol is normal, and I've lost 80 pounds. The information from class and other sources made it possible for me to obtain a good attitude in taking charge over my health. I can do all things through Christ that strengthens me. Thank you Apostle Ward for Temple Care Takers." -**Sonciare**

"I keep hearing thisbook will teach people how to live and not die! Amen." **Jennifer**

"Visualizing our bodies as God's Temple allows us to be healed spiritually, mentally, emotionally and physically. Taking Care of the Temple gives you specific instructions in accomplishing this. If you follow these instructions, it will be impossible for your body not to improve. It has been fun working through the manual with the TCT group to maximize my health by learning new ways to live. May you enjoy the benefits that good health brings. I thank God that he chose Julie to impart this wisdom to us." -**Mom aka Shirley J. Stephen**

"I found the meetings of the Temple Care Takers to be uplifting and motivational. They provided support and the framework to understand how valuable our bodies are and how God intended for us to care for them. Thank you for offering this blessing and wonderful opportunity to share and fellowship." -**Lenore**

Introduction

Imagine your body being the temple of God. The temple in the Old Testament was said to have housed the very presence of God in the Holy of Holies. Well, now that Jesus has redeemed us back to the Father by His blood, we are that temple. Wow, think about that! If you have difficulty grasping that, look at what the Word of God says regarding it in 1 Corinthians 3:16-17 (KJV). It reads:

"16 Know ye not that ye are the temple of God, and that the Spirit of God dwelleth in you? 17 If any man defile the temple of God, him shall God destroy; for the temple of God is holy, which temple ye are."

The Word of God has settled the fact that your body is indeed considered the temple of God.

The American Tract Society Dictionary defines temple as: "A building hallowed by the special presence of God, and consecrated to His worship." The distinctive idea of a temple, contrasted with all other buildings, is that it is the dwelling place of a deity; and every heathen temple had its idol, but the true and living God dwelt "between the cherubim" in the Holy of Holies at Jerusalem.

Knowledge that our body is "hallowed," housing His "special presence" and consecrated to His worship, brings to light a lot of things. To understand these things let's first look at the definition of "hallowed." According to Eason's 1897 Bible Dictionary, it means, "to render sacred, to consecrate (Ex. 28:38; 29:1)." This word is from the Saxon, and properly means "to make holy." The name of God is "hallowed," i.e., is reverenced as holy (Matthew 6:9).

This means we cannot just do whatever we want to do with our bodies. Most of the time, believers tend to not want to discuss what they do with their bodies. We usually yield to the flesh and put in it and on it whatever we desire. If you are struggling with smoking cigarettes, the Holy Spirit will help you get free to begin taking care of your temple. The same holds true for drugs and alcohol addictions. If you've been delivered from alcohol, drugs, cigarettes, illicit sex, etc. you may feel that you are taking care of your temple, but this is not necessarily so. Are you rendering your body to the Holy Spirit, asking Him what you need to be doing? Is your temple up to Kingdom Code? Are you in tip top physical shape so that God's Kingdom is being manifested in your life? Or are you making do, not really feeling well but glad that you are able to get up and about? There is so much more God wants for us!

When the Father began to deal with me regarding taking care of His temple I struggled quite a bit. For one, I was about 50 lbs overweight. I struggled with allergies, chronic bronchitis and constipation just to name a few maladies- but most of all I loved sugar. I could live off of eating nothing but sweets, homemade rolls, lots of cheese and other processed foods. But then one day one of my loved ones received a diagnosis that required a total lifestyle change, and I needed to support them by changing my eating habits right along with them. So, there we were- almost vegans. We ate absolutely no sweets and no meat other than a very occasional grilled salmon. I walked in that for about six months before falling off the wagon. All it took was a very hungry moment and a fabulous smelling and delicious looking turkey sandwich and I plunged right back into my horrible eating habits.

The mercy and grace of God remained with me and I honestly felt like I didn't have any real problems. The Lord would speak to me on occasion about the damage I was doing to my body and that there were multitudes of His leaders that were just as bound that He wanted to set free. This went on for quite some time until I began noticing that I was having more and more difficulty breathing and coughing without being able to control it as I had in the past. Then came the day that the Lord gave me a very serious warning; this is what He said to me:

"My daughter this is the time of renewing your health-this must be your focus. You must focus on this, it is related to life. You can't just eat anything. This is a warning you must obey Me in this thing. Run away from the things you should not have as if it were a poison. When you see things I have told you to avoid, look at them as if they are poison and will cause premature death. If you leave this earth before time it will be because you disobeyed in this area. The enemy would love to take you out early, but he cannot unless you disobey Me in this area. It is important!"

I would like to say that I immediately got on my healthy path, but I didn't. My loved one lost her battle with breast cancer and went home to be with the Lord. I continued on not taking care of my temple properly and when I went to the doctors, I found that I was not only overweight, but I had diabetes and high blood pressure as well.

I had not heeded the warning of the Lord. I continued to eat poorly, didn't get adequate rest and didn't properly hydrate my body. I had shared my idea of Taking Care of the Temple with others and every time they saw me they inquired about my Temple Care Taking idea.

I began having workshops and saw that what God had given me could really work if put into practice. With the help of the Holy Spirit and prayer, I am no longer addicted to the white powder (white sugar that is). The funny thing is, sugar is considered a drug by those that have researched and studied the effects. There are many good books that teach on this so I won't stay on this (see Notes/Reference, Sugar: Toxic Invader #1). Instead, we will focus on how to take care of this wonderful temple the Lord has called us to be stewards over. The Bible talks about being good stewards of the things He has entrusted us with, so purpose in your heart and pray along with me that you will become a good caretaker of the temple of God, also known as your body. *Let's get started!*

Temple Care Takers
Promoting Optimum Health

We have a Father who is a God of action and a God of order, and He wants us to take care of the temple He has given us to use while walking this earth. We are a triune being (spirit, soul and body) and each must be healthy for us to be whole.

3 John 1:2 says: "Beloved, I pray that you may prosper in all things and be in health, just as your soul prospers."

Temple Care Takers find the healthy path, get well, and maintain balance in their lives. Some questions to ponder:

- *What does healthy lifestyle changes mean to me?*
- *What changes do I want to see in my health?*
- *What do I think I need to do in order to become a good Temple Care Taker?*
- *If you could have anything you desired related to your health what would it be?*

Before beginning the journey of taking care of your temple, you must decide that you are going to be successful in getting your temple to the state God intended it to be- which I call *"up to Kingdom Code"*- with the help of the Holy Spirit.

First, let us agree in prayer with the Holy Spirit confessing what the Word says about the temple of God in 2 Corinthians 6:16, *"And what agreement hath the temple of God with idols? For ye are the temple of the living God; as God hath said, I will dwell in them, and walk in them; and I will be their God, and they shall be my people."*

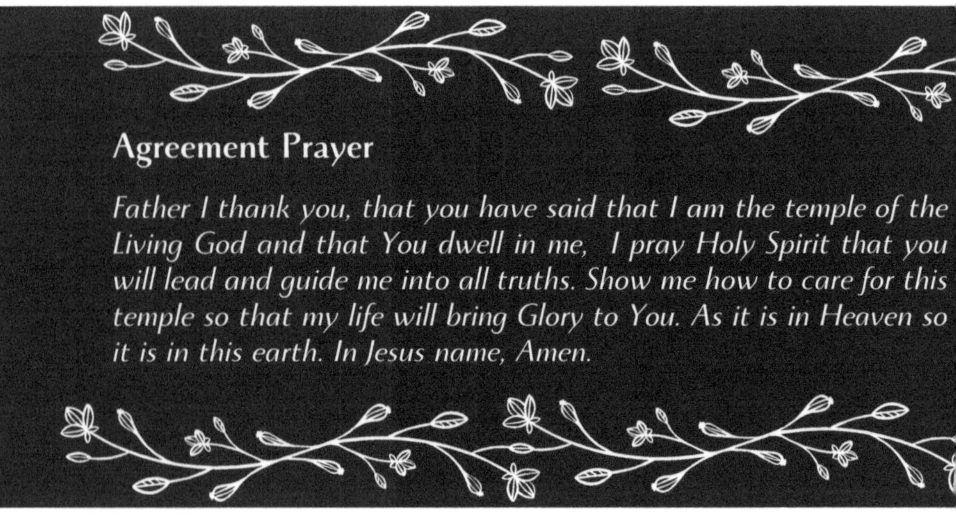

Yes, it's that simple. Just ask the Holy Spirit to help you and He will. The Word says in Proverbs 3: 5- 6, *"Trust in the LORD with all thine heart; and lean not unto thine own understanding. In all thy ways acknowledge Him, and He shall direct thy paths."*

So just trust in the Lord with everything within you and don't pay any attention to your logic or way of thinking because it won't get you the desired results. Before doing anything, acknowledge the Lord- (meaning ask Him what you need to do)- then He will guide you in all things. This scripture doesn't mean give a nod to God and then do what you want to do; it means just what it says. Don't do anything unless He tells you to do it! That blind obedience will keep you safe in His will.

Getting Started

Set A Start Date

The first thing you should do is set a start date for your first day on the path to taking care of your temple. Give yourself enough time to prepare, otherwise you will set yourself up for failure and the accuser of the brethren will accuse you again as he always does. Instead of vaguely vowing to do better, pick an exact date to get started on taking care of your temple, as being specific makes you less likely to procrastinate.

Start A Journal

After setting a start date, get a journal. Get one that you won't mind getting messy because it will go with you EVERYWHERE. This journal will be multi-purpose. You will use it to take note of the things that the Holy Spirit tells you and it will also be a food log. The food log will include what you eat, what you wanted to eat, what you almost ate, etc. After completing your pre-work up assignments (see Appendix: Assignments), you will note the following in your journal:

A. List all known physical problems after completing the **Body Questionnaire (Treelite)**.

B. List all of the emotions you experience during the lifestyle changes.

C. Note any mild detoxification symptoms (i.e. headaches, fatigue, flu-like symptoms, nausea, etc.)

D. Note changes in your energy levels.

E. Note the cessation of any physical problems that you noted earlier.

F. Write down all the goals you have achieved.

G. Jot down all the healthy living roadblocks you might encounter and then brainstorm for excuse extinguishers. Note what you can do to counteract every excuse you listed as a barrier to healthy living.

Prepare Your Kitchen

Adapt your kitchen to be Temple Care Taker (TCT) friendly.

A. Organize your refrigerator, pantry, cabinets, and cupboards. Put the things that support TCT TM at eye-level.

B. Remove all things that aren't supporters of TCT, including:
- Fatty Meats
- Processed Foods
- White Sugar (SAD-Standard American Diet)
- Fried Foods
- Canned Goods (Excluding Low Sodium)
- Salty Foods (Chips, etc.)
- Carbonated Sodas (Diet & Regular)

C. Replace everything removed with fresh fruit and vegetables (organic if at all possible), unsalted nuts, etc.

8

Partner with the Holy Spirit & A Friend

When you connect with the Holy Spirit He will speak to you and encourage you to do the right thing. What will also assist you is a person in the flesh that you will be responsible to. It has been proven with research that people do better when they have support, so you will need that also. It will be very beneficial if you pull in your prayer partner, friend or family member to be your support as well, then they can become a Temple Care Taker too!

Saturate & Soak Your Mind

A. *Saturate and soak your mind* with information about your body, what foods to eat and those to avoid.

B. *Saturate and soak your mind* with positive thoughts- you can do it! (Philippians 4:13)

C. *Saturate and soak your mind* with confessions of what the Word of God says that you are and that you can do.

Get Your TCT, Instruments & Cleaning Products

You should invest in the following items:

A. Juicer

B. Supplements

C. Fiber, colonic cleansers, ets.

Plan Your Meals

Write out a meal plan every week; include breakfast, mid-morning snack, lunch, mid-afternoon snack, and dinner. Eat enough and on time so you won't be hungry and crave all the wrong foods. You will find that when you start eating the right foods, you can eat a lot more and not gain a lot of weight. Find good healthy food choices at restaurants for occasional nights out.

Plan Movement Into Your Schedule

Walk everyday for a minimum of 20 -30 minutes. You can walk around your home, around the mall (don't spend all your money!) or a nice neighborhood park. Wherever you choose, just be sure to move around; don't be sedentary. This is a very important part of taking care of your temple. It is also an area that the Lord says most of His children are lacking in. We are really lazy! Yes, I said we because I am a Temple Caretaker in process. If you don't want to walk, put on your favorite praise music and dance and praise the Lord. That way, you will have incorporated movement along with worship into your life. When you go to work or to the mall don't pray for a close spot, park further away from the door.

TCT Modules In A Nutshell

The Bible tells us first natural then spiritual. We must rein our body in and discipline and buffet it to get in line with the Word in the natural. If you apply the Word and pray both the natural and the spiritual will fall in line.

"However, the spiritual [the immortal life] is not first, but the physical [the mortal life]; then the spiritual."
-1 Corinthians 15:46

T- Take
A-Action
C-Cleanse and
K-Kindle a Love for Detoxifying
L-Load and Rebuild Your Nutritional Systems
E-Extending Life by Adding Antioxidants Daily

There are seven modules in the process of becoming a Temple Care Taker.

Module I   Reflections/Taking Inventory

Module II   Removing the Rubbish/Detoxification

Module III   Rebuilding from the Inside Out

Module IV   Restoration

Module V   Renovation

Module VI   Refreshing/Reflection

Module VII Remaining

If you become a TCT partner and join in on conference calls, there will be discussions on each of the modules with movement plans, scripture and prayer. There will also be TCT coaches and team leaders called PEERS (Prayer Partners to Encourage, Empower, Reinforce and Support) available to encourage and exhort you on your healthy path.

Module 1

Reflections/Taking Inventory

We are a three part being. In order to properly care for our temple, we must be cognizant of this and address our spirit and soul as well as our body.

This module is about evaluating:

1) Your spiritual status and deciding what you want to do about it.
2) Your environment (which affects your emotional and mental status) and deciding what you want to do about it.
3) Your physical status and deciding what you want to do about it.

Some questions to ponder:

Spirit: Describe your relationship with the Heavenly Father. How often do you pray and seek the face of the Father? How often do you read and/or study the Word? How often are you praying, interceding, worshipping, and obeying the voice of the Lord? Do you know and understand the voice of the Lord? How long has He been telling you to change how you care for His temple? Do you find time everyday to sit and hear what He has to say to you? Not just bombarding Him with your needs, and other people's needs, but actually sitting still and listening to whatever He wants to say to you. These are some of the things that you can elaborate on in your journal. It is important that each day you write down whatever the Holy Spirit says to you and then review what He said at the end of the week.

Soul: Describe the state of your emotions. What areas are you struggling with in your mind, will and emotions? Do you need deliverance from generational curses? Do you have family members that struggle with the same things you do- like overeating, eating the wrong things, drinking alcohol, using drugs, etc?

Take note of your family inheritance because those are areas that you will need deliverance in. Taking care of the temple will involve being delivered from family iniquity and unclean spirits that have held you in bondage. Make note of the things you need deliverance from in your journal and then you and your TCT coach/team leader can address them when you meet or perhaps you can discuss them with your prayer partner or pastor. Deliverance will be an ongoing process throughout all of the modules.

Body: How would you describe your physical well being? What is the actual state of your body? What size do you really wear? Not what you tell others, but what is the truth of the matter? How do you feel about your body? How are you taking care of your hair, your skin, your hands/nails and your feet right now? What problems are you encountering in your body? Are you addicted to any foods? Caffeine (the respectable addiction)? Sugar? Meat or cheese? Bread? This is the time to note in your journal the truth of the matter. There are several quizzes for you to take- Caffeine survey, Detox Quiz and Your Sugar Risk Quiz and they will help you decipher if you are indeed addicted. The Lord already knows what's going on and He is the only one that can help us be what we need to be to have His Kingdom established in our lives.

There is a Body Systems Questionnaire prepared by "The Tree of Light Publishing" website (**www.treelite.com**) that you can complete to help you take inventory of your physical status. This questionnaire will give you a good picture of what your actual physical status is. Please visit this website for more information and education. After doing so it will point out the areas in your body that you will need to concentrate on to restore your temple to the state that is desired of the Holy Spirit. If you join the TCT website you will be given a TACKLE Plan so you can actively engage in addressing your nutritional deficits.

Take Inventory:

1.) What do you want?

2.) What is the state of your health now?

3.) What do you have to do to achieve what you want?

For example: Change Eating Habits, Detox, Get Supplements, Colonics, 2-Week Liver Support, Incorporate Rest, Massages, Fasting, Exercise, Movement, Walking, etc.

What will it take to bring my temple into Kingdom Code? While walking the healthy path I will consider my temple to be in restoration, renovation mode or in the process of attaining Kingdom Code. What do you consider to be healthy? What image comes to mind? First of all, we are made in the image of God and you can do all things through Christ, so don't be discouraged. When you journal think about what you have discovered about yourself and decide what you want to do about it. You may use the daily log (Appendix) to keep track of everything you eat for 3 days to help you get a better picture of your eating habits. To get started: make your plans, execute your plans, evaluate your plans, and then make new plans.

Prayer

Father in the name of Jesus, Your Word tells me to acknowledge you in all my ways and you will direct my path. I understand in order to get my body up to Kingdom Code I need to find out what areas are in deficit and follow your instructions regarding what to do. I ask you Holy Spirit to help me stay consistent to the process as you reveal the true state of my temple. In Jesus name I pray, Amen.

Module 2
Removing the Rubbish/Detoxification

Spirit: "Since we have these promises, dear friends, let us purify ourselves from everything that contaminates body and spirit, perfecting holiness out of reverence for God."- **2 Corinthians 7:1**

Repent (*see confession scriptures*) as the Spirit leads. *Read Psalm 51.*

Soul: Detox your soul with laughter, and remove toxic people from your space. Seek the Lord for deliverance from gluttony, disobedience, etc. Forgive and release all people who have wounded you from every offense. Shake yourself free from bad memories of past experiences. Renounce the spirit name of *"memory recall"* which causes a person to remember experiences of hurt, pain and rejection. Confess these prayers:

Father in Jesus name, I loose myself from the effects of all the bad memories, painful memories and memories of the past that would hinder me in the present or future, Amen.

Father in the name of the Lord Jesus Christ by the authority given to me to bind and loose, I loose my emotions from every evil spirit that has come in as a result of experiences of the past. I loose myself from all hurt, deep hurt, pain, sadness, grief, anger, hatred, rage, bitterness, fear and found and blocked emotions. I command these spirits to come out and I decree freedom to my emotions in the name of the Lord Jesus Christ, Amen.

Body: Make a decision to detox your body and decide that even when you begin to eat some of the items you are temporarily removing again, purpose in your heart to become more disciplined than you have been in regards to what you put in your body. Remove junk food from your life, replace soda pop with water, decrease or totally eliminate coffee (no more than 1 cup per day) eat a liver cleanse support diet (see Appendix for foods to eat), get regular colonics and enemas, increase fiber intake, engage in body brushing, decrease fried foods, cut out white sugar and do the master cleanse diet(see Stanley Burroughs) just to name a few things.

What is Detoxification?

Simply put, a detox routine is an all natural method of "cleaning out your pipes" by providing your body with the time and conditions it can use to rebuild and heal. There are many different detox routines in the world of natural health including: water fasting, juice fasting, herbal detox, detox baths and colon cleansing.

Our bodies are naturally detoxifying 24 hours a day, seven days a week. The organs involved in detoxing the body are the liver, kidneys, lymphatic system, skin, lungs and bowels. Without this system we would not survive, but living in an environment that has become more and more toxic makes it difficult for our bodies system to keep up. If your body can't eliminate all toxins, it stores it in your fatty tissues.

Factors Important to Detoxify & Improve Health

- Proper Nutrition
- Lots of Pure Water
- Walking/Exercise
- Rest (Physical & Emotional)
- Sunshine (Vitamin D)
- Fresh air

When detoxing with juicing and fasting you may experience some negative detox symptoms like: headache, sore muscles, achiness, sleep disturbances and cranky moods. These are temporary and after a couple of days you will usually start feeling better. If you are a heavy coffee drinker you will probably experience a caffeine withdrawal headache but it will soon go away. When you return to drinking coffee just limit the number of cups you drink daily.

The positive effects of detoxing outweigh the negative. You will begin to have more energy, think more clearly, exercise and move around more easily, have improved sleep and just feel better all around.

Begin making lifestyle changes and fast periodically to cleanse and maintain your health. Bragg's has a Master Cleanse drink that has all ingredients (apple vinegar cider, honey, lemon and cayenne pepper) you only need to add water. As with all cleanses, please confer with your health provider before taking.

Taking a detox bath once a week goes a long way in helping you to relax and get rid of some of your everyday stress. For about 20 minutes sit in a hot bath that contains a handful of Epsom Salt, ten drops of lavender essential oil and a half cup of baking soda. This combination draws out toxins, lowers stress levels and balances your PH levels.

The lymphatic system is important because it bathes our body's cells and carries the body's cellular waste away from the tissues to the blood which is then filtered through the liver and kidneys. To help keep the lymph flowing smoothly see *"Ways to Keep Lymphatic System Flowing Smoothly"* in Appendix.

Prayer

Father in the name of Jesus, I thank you that your Word says that as I confess my sin that you will cleanse me from all unrighteousness. So I repent for not taking care of my temple and ask you to forgive me and help me to be cleansed, and made whole in spirit, soul and body. Help me Holy Spirit to gain control of my eating habits, to get a grip on unhealthy emotions, and to remove toxic things and people out of my space. In Jesus name, Amen.

Module 3
Rebuilding from the Inside Out

Spirit: Confess the Word, re: your situation, 2-3x daily. Select scriptures specific to your needs, i.e. healing, weight/appetite scriptures, etc. I've provided some in the Appendix that you can choose from.

Soul: Confess what the Word says about you 2-3x daily. Confess scriptures like Psalm 139:14 which says, "I praise you because I am fearfully and wonderfully made; your works are wonderful, I know that full well."

Body: Implement the following into your diet: supplements, multi-vitamins, minerals, probiotics, green juice, carrot juice, water with lemon, etc. Smoothies (see in Reference, the book, J.J. Smoothies) salads everyday, and decrease meat intake to 1x per day for a few weeks.

Having a healthy temple may seem unattainable to you right now. However, the truth is no matter what condition you are currently in-spirit, soul and body- you can replenish your well-being by partnering with the Holy Spirit to do the work to bring your temple into Kingdom Code. Research indicates that within a year, 98% of the cells in your body will die and be replaced, even your brain renews itself. With the ongoing cycles of cells being replaced this means that each and every day your body can be rebuilding itself to be much better and stronger.

We have been given an *amazing body* that renews itself with *whatever material* we give it to work with.

The body needs fiber, antioxidants, vitamins, minerals and phytonutrients. Fruits and vegetables are concentrated sources of phytonutrients; other plant foods like whole grains, legumes/beans, nuts and seeds, and herbs and spices also contain phytonutrients. Green Smoothies are excellent sources of food to help rebuild your body from the inside out. *Please refer to the reference page discussing J.J's Smoothies.* Periodically, the author of the book will have ten day Smoothie Campaigns, so please refer to her Facebook page for more information if you are interested.

It's important to also be aware that a true green smoothie consists of about 60% organic fruits and 40% organic leafy greens (and sometimes a cup of liquid and organic protein powder) that is blended in a high power blender. Unlike pre-made smoothies or green juices you see for sale, green smoothies are a complete food.

Eating Healthy

Eating healthy doesn't have to be an all or nothing effort. Starting new, healthy habits takes practice and patience. Increase your intake of fruits, vegetables and grains and decrease your intake of sweets, meats, and fast foods. If you have health concerns related to diabetes be careful of fruit intake. If you eat meat and dairy products, choose leaner meats and instead of having meat with each meal, start having a meatless meal once a week. Healthy eating also means not eating too much sugar, fat, or fast foods. You can still have dessert and treats now and then. The goal is moderation.

That is after you are no longer addicted to sugar, meats and fat. If you make a decision that you will supply your body with healthy materials, it will replace damaged cells with new healthy cells. But if you continue to give it what you have been giving it, it will give you the same thing you have had.

Retraining Your Appetite

It is important to recognize when you are hungry or if emotionally you are craving certain foods because of stress or emotional issues. Start retraining your appetite by following these simple exercises. Ask yourself: Am I hungry or thirsty? If you think you're hungry, before getting something to eat, drink a full glass of water. Wait for 10 to 15 minutes then see if your stomach is growling and you have a strong urge to eat. Next, be sure to always eat breakfast. Instead of eggs, bacon, hash browns, toast, orange juice and coffee, try a nice bowl of oatmeal with some fruit and nuts. You will be surprised to find that the oatmeal will keep you fuller and more satisfied longer because of the fiber. And finally, eat smaller portions more frequently. Eat every 2-3 hours, this will help speed up your metabolism and keep you from eating too much at one time.

Prayer

Father in the name of Jesus, I thank you for this miraculous body that you have given me that is able to rebuild and regenerate itself. I ask you Father to give me the strength and fortitude to put in my body the healthy nutrients it needs to rebuild my temple into Kingdom Code. With your help I can do all things. In Jesus name, Amen.

Module 4
Restoration

Spirit: Find a quiet space, close your eyes, focus your breathing and talk to the Lord and/or meditate on Scriptures. The book of Psalms is especially inspiring. Express your gratitude. Tell the Heavenly Father daily how grateful you are for life; be still and write down what you hear the Father say to you in a journal, show your love and gratitude to family and friends by sending little notes letting them know how much you appreciate them. Read/study the Word 15 minutes per day. Read and confess daily *"Who I am in Christ"* *(See Appendix).*

Soul: Don't be a garbage can. What has been stolen from you? Are you full of worry? Jot down the things that are concerning you then brain storm ways to cope. If it continues, take authority over those thoughts and replace them with what God says about you. Say what you want until you see what you want *(See Daily Confessions in Appendix).* Find some books to build up your self-esteem; spend some time everyday exposing your mind to new information. What have you done lately that YOU wanted to do? Not what you needed to do or what other people needed you to do. The scripture says in Psalm 139:14, *"You are fearfully and wonderfully made,. marvelous are thy works; and that my soul knoweth right well."* Does your soul (your mind, will and emotions) BELIEVE that you are fearfully and wonderfully made? Look at the motives-do you do things for people because you want to be accepted? Or loved? Think about that.

Body: Begin taking care of your hair, skin nails, etc. Rest: stay in the bed longer. Do you have difficulty relaxing or resting? Try deep breathing exercises *(see Appendix)*. Perhaps you can add fasting to your regimen. Fasting has many physical and spiritual benefits. Fasting helps you lose weight because it allows the body to burn fat cells more effectively than just regular dieting. Fasting speeds up your metabolism by giving your digestive system a rest. This may possibly energize your metabolism to burn calories more efficiently.

It has also been found that fasting helps to promote healthier bowel function. The Bible gives many examples of fasting. Daniel fasted from the rich foods of the Babylonians and after doing so was found to be healthier than all of the others that ate the rich unhealthy foods. Perhaps a Daniel Fast will help you gain better control of your appetite and eating habits. Maybe give it a try for a day at a time. See the Appendix for foods that can be eaten while on a Daniel Fast as well as the Liver Support Diet (Dr. Don Colbert *"Toxic Relief"*). Begin to rest in who you are in Christ, keep doing the things you have learned in Modules 2 and 3. Have faith, believe and trust that because you have submitted to the Holy Spirit to help you bring your temple into Kingdom Code, and you want His will done in your earth (your body) as it is in Heaven, that it will be done.

Prayer

Father in the name of Jesus, I thank you for this time of restoration. As I meditate and confess Your Word I will see the manifestation of a healthy and strong soul and spirit man. As I detox and rebuild my body, exercising restraint and discipline, I will see the manifestation of a stronger, healthier body. In Jesus name, Amen.

Module 5
Renovation

Spirit: Build up! Regain ground stolen by the enemy, tear down strongholds and replace them with godly strongholds. Read and confess daily "TCT Kingdom Prayers/Affirmations" (*See Appendix*).

Soul: Rebuild relationships that have been torn down through lack of attention, Call and check on someone you have been thinking about and tell them you love them; send a note (email) to someone and tell them you love them and are praying for them; go for a walk with an old friend or family member. Make peace with yourself... your thighs, your face, your hair, or whatever about yourself that you have tried to change but haven't been successful at. Make peace with yourself and say, *"I am who I am, and I will do my best and leave the rest to you God. Rejection will not rule over me. I am who God says I am, and I can do what God says I can do."*

Body: Before starting a workout regimen, check with your healthcare professional who can tell you which regimen would be best for you based on your medical history. Look for enjoyable ways to fit exercise into your routine-even if it's only 20 minutes or so. Walking is usually acceptable for most people. However, if you don't have time to do a 30 minute power walk, how about trying three 10 minute walks instead? Increase movement in your lifestyle by walking while talking on the cell phone, and during lunch time. In order to be motivated to increase movement, you need to decide what kind of movement you enjoy. Choose a workout that you will enjoy- water aerobics, Zumba, fitness boxing, swimming or even gardening. Any kind of movement will be beneficial. Set realistic goals.

Don't begin by saying you will work out 45 minutes every day. Your life is probably full with the many hats you wear so don't set yourself up for failure by reaching too high. Set short term goals to increase your own fitness level, like walking 15-30 minutes, 2-3 times a week. You will be encouraged by attaining your short-term goals. Move with a friend, this will make you accountable to someone else and accountability is a much more powerful motivator than willpower. Change up your workout, maybe walk one day, go to a Zumba class another day, and go to water aerobics another day. Doing this will keep your movement regimen fresh.

Prayer

Father in the name of Jesus, I thank you that you have provided me with the ability to move this amazing body that you have given me. Holy Spirit, please teach and motivate me to increase movement so that my stamina and energy will be increased. In Jesus name, Amen.

Module 6
Refreshing/Reflection

Have you achieved your goals? Are you satisfied with the results of walking the health path? What barriers or obstacles did you encounter?

Spirit: Worship- Give thanks for what has been done, reflect on His goodness.

Soul: Reflect on how blessed you are. What improvements do you see in your emotions and mindset?

Body: Get a massage- have a pamper party or lay in the sun and do nothing.

Let's reflect on what we've learned so far. In order to know what needs to be done, we must assess or take inventory of what condition our temple is in. If our temple is in need of cleansing we must do what is necessary to get it cleansed/detoxed. Then, after cleansing our temple, we need to rebuild, restore, replenish and renovate whatever has been depleted. See the next page for steps.

Reflection of Temple Care Taking

1. **Take a daily multi-vitamin to support your body's nutritional needs.**

2. **Eat protein, healthy fats and complex carbohydrates for breakfast-** simple carbs and sugar fire up your insulin receptors and spark these sugar cravings. Starting your day with a sugary or high carb breakfast dooms you to a day of up and down blood sugar levels, which will drive you to eat too much of the wrong things all day long.

3. **Shop the perimeter of your grocery store—avoid the processed foods in the center aisles.** Read all labels and be wary of food that contains aspartame, neotame, saccharin, acesulfame K, or sucralose. No studies have been done on the safety of eating artificial sweeteners and who wants to become a living, breathing test subject? So if you consume them, do so prudently.

4. **Minimize or avoid products that have sugar, high-fructose corn syrup or corn syrup near the top of their ingredient list.** Sugar can also be disguised as evaporated cane juice, cane sugar, beet sugar, glucose, sucrose, maltose, maltodextrin, dextrose, sorbitol, fructose, corn sugar, fruit juice concentrate, barley malt, caramel, and carob syrup.

5. **Keep a bowl of fresh ripe fruit nearby to snack on to relieve your sugar cravings.** Think primitive and eat fruit that is in season. The fresher the fruit, the more succulent and satisfying it will be. You may find you don't need anything sweeter.

6. **If you are craving something sweet, don't feel guilty.** We're often made to feel that avoiding sugar is only a matter of willpower, but it's more complicated than that. Most of the time, uncontrollable or patterned cravings stem from a malfunctioning metabolism or low serotonin. Work on healthy nutrition and you'll find your cravings will disappear.

7. **Indulge yourself sometimes.** We have sweet taste buds for a reason. Try a piece of fruit first- you may find your craving diminishes. If you still want a piece of chocolate or pie, go ahead. But savor it slowly like a rare treat you may not have again for a while. Once your brain is allowed to fully register the experience, you may find you're satisfied after a few bites. To help balance out the accompanying insulin surge, eat a piece of protein with it. Just make it a treat, not a habit.

8. **Take a short walk after eating and breathe in deeply.**

9. **Focus more on what you'd like to cook and eat, than what you shouldn't.** If you listen to your body, it may surprise you with a craving for eggs instead of a diet soda.

Prayer

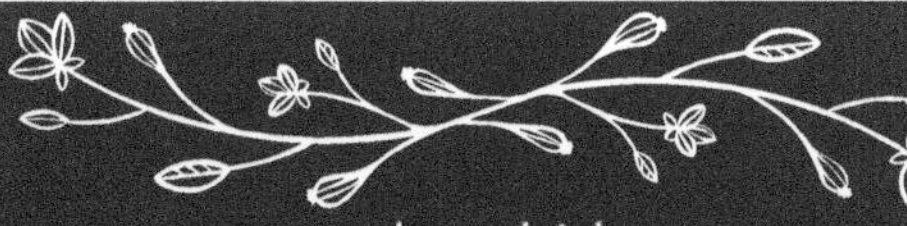

Father God in the name of Jesus, You are my strength and I lean on you. My ability to stay committed to healthy eating and taking care of my temple comes from you. Help me to maintain the will power I need to eliminate sugar and empty calories from my diet. Give me the focus I need to implement all that I am learning. Father God, replace any discouragement with hope and any doubt with faith. I thank You Lord for seeing me through and bringing my body into Kingdom Code in Jesus name, Amen.

Module 7
Remaining

Set a regimen of prayer, reading, and studying the Word. Also do the following:

1. **Confession**- Don't stuff things down, address them.

2. **Body**- Stick with what you've learned.

3. **Join a TCT Group**- TCT groups provide online support as well as free webinars and conference calls on various health and ministry subject matters.

Identify one thing this month that could sabotage your health goals and change that routine. If watching TV triggers mindless eating, make a schedule of when you will watch TV, and never for more than 1-2 hours daily. Think of some healthy, fun things to do. Also do the following:

- To maintain divine health and feel good every day, start the seven modules over.

- Take inventory of your spirit, soul, and body.

- Remove anything that isn't producing good things in your life.

- Rebuild from the inside out.

- Restore anything that has been lost.

- Renovate anything that needs fixing. Reflect/Refresh, and Remain in divine health, and a good Temple Care Taker.

- Eat a healthy whole food diet comprised of clean, organic (when possible) foods from both the plant and animal kingdom. Avoid packaged and junk food. At least 50% of your intake should be fruit and vegetables.

- Exercise and/or walk for at least 30 minutes every day. Alternate between aerobics/Zumba (brisk walking) and weight training.

- Spend at least 10 minutes in the direct sunshine every day.

- Drink filtered or purified water. The recommended amount is 6-8 glasses daily. If you must drink soda pop, condition yourself to drink the 6-8 glasses of water before drinking anything else. Your desire for the soda pop will lessen.

Note: *Persons with kidney or heart issues should follow the fluid allowances recommended by your healthcare providers.*

- Begin juicing and drink 16 ounces of fresh vegetable juices (i.e. carrot/apple, etc.) whenever possible.

- Snack on living food like fruits and veggies instead of junk foods.

- Breathe the purest air possible. Don't tolerate any one smoking in your space.

- Meditate on the Word of God for at least 30 minutes daily to remove stress and receive instructions for your day.

- Laugh and spend time with friends and/or family. God wants you to be happy and enjoy your life.

- Research and study information on the internet to learn more about taking care of the temple of God.

- Join Temple Care Takers when you send an email to, **wearetemplecaretakers@gmail.com** with "Join TCT" in the subject line, and you will be registered as a member.

The information provided by "Temple Care Takers" is for educational purposes only and IS NOT intended as a substitute for professional medical advice, diagnosis, or treatment. Always seek professional medical advice from your physician or other qualified healthcare provider with any questions you may have regarding a medical condition.

Detox Quiz

Take this detox cleanse quiz by Lysabeth Lopez to determine if you are toxic. Check ALL symptoms that apply to you. If you check three or more of these symptoms you may need a cleanse. Visit her website at http://trainwithlyzabeth.com/detox-cleanse-quiz/.

- [ ] Cravings for carbs, starches, sugar, salt and breads
- [ ] Have bloating and gas, especially after meals
- [ ] Easily retain water
- [ ] Distended lower abdomen
- [ ] Acne
- [ ] Bad bread and foul body odor
- [ ] Headaches
- [ ] Joint pain and stiffness
- [ ] Overall lethargy, fatigue and feeling sluggish
- [ ] Dry skin, nails and hair; eczema
- [ ] Depression
- [ ] Decreased libido
- [ ] Irritability
- [ ] Constipation and/or diarrhea (overall irregularity)
- [ ] Mood Swings & PMS
- [ ] Lack of concentration
- [ ] Weakened immunity and frequent colds
- [ ] Weight gain and difficulty losing weight

Sugar Addiction Quiz

Are you a sugar addict? Answer these 20 questions with yes or no answers to find out.

1. Do you experience a sense of euphoria, excitement or relief when you eat sweets?

2. Do you feel like sugar has a magical control over you?

3. Does eating sweets make you happy even when you have a bad day?

4. Have you ever traveled far, gone out late at night, or overcome obstacles in order to get or purchase sugary snacks?

5. Do you feel guilty after eating sweet foods?

6. Is eating something sugary a planned part of your everyday schedule?

7. Do you routinely eat sweets when you are alone?

8. Do you find yourself thinking about what sweets you will try next?

9. Do you or your family make and/or stockpile sugary snacks and desserts?

10. Does your energy feel depleted as a result of eating too much sugar?

11. Have you ever tried (and failed) to limit the amount of sugar you eat?

12. Do you experience physical reactions when you go without sweets for a long period of time?

13. Do you lie about or hide the amount of sugar you eat?

14. Do you worry that eating sugar will damage your health, but you keep eating it anyway?

15. Do you have trouble waking up in the morning and then find yourself crashing in the afternoon?

16. Do you have crust in the corner of your eyes when you wake up in the morning?

17. If you are left alone with a box of your favorite sweet snack, would you eat the whole thing until it's gone?

18. Is a celebration not a celebration unless sweets are involved?

19. Do you ever sacrifice eating good food to instead eat a meal made of sugar?

20. Is loving sweet foods part of your personality so much so that friends would describe you as someone who loves sugar?

If you answered yes to 3 or less questions, it appears that you are not having major issues with sugary sweets. Stay healthy and be well.

If you answered yes to 4 to 6 questions, sugar is a player in your life so be aware of what you eat. Remember, addictions start as small habits that spiral out of control. It never hurts to reduce sweets.

If you answered yes to 7 or more questions, sugar is a big part of your life. Try cutting out all sweets from your diet for one month and see how you feel. This is the first step to understanding the role sugar plays in your everyday life.

Caffeine Habit or Addiction Survey

What role does caffeine play in your life? Below are some questions that will help you recognize whether caffeine is a habit, dependence or an addiction for you.

1. Can you start the day without a cup of coffee?

2. Do you usually have a second cup before lunch?

3. Does it bother you if you miss your mid-morning or mid-afternoon coffee break?

4. Do you drink more coffee when under stress?

5. Do you consume more than 250 milligrams of caffeine every day?

6. If you've ever gone a whole day without coffee or other caffeinated drinks did you:
   - Feel dramatically different?
   - Did you drink more coffee the next day?
   - Did you have a headache?

7. Do you always choose a coffee, tea or cola that has caffeine rather than one that doesn't?

8. Do you regularly experience more than two of the recognized symptoms of caffeinism? (Insomnia, depression, irritability, chronic fatigue, restlessness)

9. Do you depend on coffee to make you feel good?

10. Do you think it's impossible to face the day without coffee?

If you answered yes to 5 or more questions you may be dependent on caffeine. It's not a healthy habit and can be just as hard to quit as smoking. But...you're definitely not alone.

Appendix

Taking Inventory of Spirit and Soul

Soul- What areas are you struggling with in your mind, will and emotions? (i.e. depression, low self-esteem, savior complex, loneliness, emotional eating etc.) Do you have family members that struggle with the same things you do? (Generational iniquities/curses).

1. Write out areas you are struggling with.
2. Select one that is affecting you the most.
3. Write 2 SMART goals (see SMART goals in Appendix), one STG (Short-term goal, 90 days) and one LTG (Long-term goal, 6 months to 1 year).
4. Write 3 things you will do to work on each of these goals (objectives).

Spirit- Connection to the Father God. Ways we connect to the Father include: Prayer, Praise, Worship, Reading and Studying the Word of God, and Quiet Time-listening.

1. How well do you know and understand the voice of the Lord?
2. When do you find time to pray and seek the face of the Father? Not just praying regarding your needs and the needs of others?

Quiet time is sitting, being still, and listening to what He wants to say. He's always talking to us.

1. Make a STG related to one of the 5 ways we connect to the Father (See example next page).

Thoughts/Feelings

Use the area below to write out your thoughts and feelings during this assignment.

Smart Goal Example

Specific: What exactly will you accomplish?

Measurable: How will you know when you have reached this goal?

Achievable: Is achieving this goal realistic with effort and commitment? Do you have the resources to achieve this goal? If not, how will you get them?

Relevant: Why is this goal significant to your life?

Timely: When will you achieve this goal?

1 Long-term Health Goal example for TCT
- I-Lose 40 lbs in 12 months
- Specific- lose specific amount of weight (40 lbs)
- Measurable- will be 40 lbs lighter
- Achievable: 40 lbs in 12 months would be 3.33 lbs a month, less than 1 lb a week is possible.
- Relevant- Losing weight is relevant to becoming healthier and taking care of my temple.
- Timely- in 12 months.

Objectives- What you will do to accomplish this goal?

A. Increase exercise/movement to 30-45 minutes daily.

B. Follow TCT eating plan consistently.

Journaling A Path to Better Health

If you share your thoughts and feelings on Facebook, emails, twitter, YouTube or Instagram, you are participating in a form of journaling. Journaling has many benefits. For one it helps to clarify your feelings and thoughts. For example do you ever feel confused inside, unsure of what you want or feel, but if you talk to someone that allows you to express yourself you feel better? Well take a few minutes, and jot down your thoughts and emotions. Don't worry about how it sounds, nor if it's grammatically correct or if all your words are spelled correctly.

When you do this it will become clearer how you feel and what your thoughts are. Another benefit of journaling is it helps you to know yourself better. When you routinely journal you will be made aware of what makes you feel confident and happy as well as which situations in your life and the people that are toxic for you. This is crucial information for the emotional well-being of your soul (mind, will and emotions). Journaling reduces stress. When we have feelings of anger, sadness and other painful emotions, when we write it helps to release some of those feelings. It seems we feel calmer and are better able to deal with pressure filled situations. Journaling is personal and can be done in various ways.

On the next page are some suggestions, but you should find what works for you and do that.

Suggestions for Journaling

1.Set aside 15-20 minutes everyday that you will journal.

2.Start anywhere/anytime, and don't worry about spelling, punctuation or grammar.

3.Be sure to write quickly. This will free your brain from all the practical *"shoulds"* and other thoughts that block your journaling.

To help you focus, here are three questions to ponder:

1. What happened?
2. How did that make you feel?
3. Why do you think you felt that way?

TCT Assignments- Making Healthier Choices

Making healthy eating happen requires planning, shopping and preparing meals.

How to Plan

Set aside a few minutes to think of and write down the meals you'll fix the next week. Make your shopping list after asking yourself the following questions:

- What ingredients do I need to make these meals?
- What foods do I need to eat healthy breakfast, lunches, dinners and snacks?
- What foods do I already have in the house?

Make your shopping list based on your response to these questions.

1. Plan Meals for A Week
   a. You must eat breakfast every morning like a "King". Breakfast should include a protein (turkey bacon, organic eggs, etc.); fruit (orange juice with Vitamin C crystals, grapefruits, etc.); fiber (oatmeal with apples, and walnuts or almonds, grits, etc.); and tea (herb).
   b. Drink 6-8 glasses of water a day.
   c. Eat lunch like a prince.
   d. Eat dinner like a pauper.
   e. Snacks- fruit
2. Plan movement into your schedule. Put it in your planner.
   a. For 20-30 minutes, walk daily, incorporate movement with a DVD, or dance with praise music.
   b. Report movements every other day to PEERS (Prayer, Encourage, Empower, Reinforcement Support) via call or email.

3. **Remove chosen toxic foods for the week**
   a. This includes all caffeine and/or white sugar.
   b. Check out Dr. Ben Kim's Apple Detox (see notes for website).
      i. Have a meatless meal once per week.
      ii. Exchange white rice for brown rice.

Short-term/Long-term Goals (3 Health Goals) related to body questionnaire
Ex. b/p from 150/88 to less than 140/70 or lose 1-2 lbs weekly.

5. **Plan a reward for following the TCT plan.**
Ex. Pedicure, facial, manicure, massage, etc.

Our liver gets overloaded...
- From toxins in our foods (fatty meats, etc.)
- From water with too much bacteria, chemicals, heavy metals and so forth
- Digestion problems

TCT Program for Toxic Relief
1) Begin a 2-week diet to strengthen and support your liver and improve your elimination through the GI tract.
For example: Eat plenty of organic fruits, organic vegetables, and free range meats. Eat as may raw vegetables as possible, beans, live friendly starches (brown rice, wild rice, rice crackers, rice pasta etc.).
2) Go on a juice fast for 2-3 days, but before doing so, discuss with your medical provider.
3) Begin making lifestyle changes and fast periodically to continue to cleanse and maintain your health.

Assignments

☐ *Plan meals for the week*
- Start looking at portion sizes.
- Drink a glass of water before every meal.
- Don't eat any meals after 8:00PM.
- Purchase and begin to take supplements.

☐ *Plan movement into your schedule- put in planner*
- 20-30 minutes, walk daily, movement with a DVD, or dance with praise music
- Report movements every other day to PEER (email or call)

☐ *Continue to work on removing chosen toxic foods*
- All caffeine and/or white sugar
- Note in your journal how you are feeling
- Watch and make note of all your triggers

☐ *Short-term/Long-term goals (3 health goals) related to body questionnaire*
- Review what actions you noted you would do, and assess if you need to add to or change any of them.

☐ *Spend 10-15 minutes daily renewing your mind*
- Write out and think about what habits you need to change.
- Write out and think about the major factors affecting your health and well-being.

Modifying Recipes for A Healthier You
Tips to Decrease the Total Fat & Lower Calories

Instead of this:	Try using this:
Shortening, butter or oil in baking	Use applesauce or prune puree for half of the butter, shortening or oil. May need to reduce baking time by 25%.
Instead of whole milk, half and half or evaporated milk	Use skim milk, 1% milk, almond milk, evaporated skim milk.
Butter, shortening, margarine, or oil to prevent sticking	When frying foods use cooking spray, water, broth, "Earth balance" or nonstick pans.
Full fat cream cheese	Use low fat or non fat cream cheese, or low fat cottage cheese pureed until smooth.
Regular mayonnaise or salad dressing	Use low fat, reduced or non fat mayonnaise or vegenaise (with grape seed oil).
Eggs	Use egg whites (usually 2 egg whites for every egg) or ¼ cup egg substitute
Frying in fat	Use cooking methods such as bake, boil, broil, grill, poach, roast or stir-fry.

Tips to Reduce Sodium (Salt)

Instead of this:	Try using this:
Salt	Omit salt or reduce salt by ½ in most recipes (except in products with yeast). Cook foods without adding salt. Don't put the salt shaker on the table.
Frozen or canned vegetables	Choose frozen vegetables without sauces or use no-salt-added canned goods. Rinsing canned vegetables will help reduce sodium.
Seasoning salt or spice mixes with salt.	Use salt-free seasonings and spice mixes. Use herbs, spices, lemon juice, or vinegar to flavor food instead of salt. Seasonings high in sodium include catsup, chili sauce, chili powder, bouillon cubes, barbecue sauce, soy sauce, Worcestershire sauce, and meat tenderizers.

Tips to Reduce the Amount of Sugar

Instead of this:	Try using this:
Sugar	Reducing sugar by ¼ to 1/3 in baked goods and desserts. If recipe calls for 1 cup, use 2/3 cup. Cinnamon, vanilla, and almond extract can be added to give impression of sweetness. Do not remove all sugar in yeast breads as sugar provides food for the yeast.
Syrup	Pureed fruit, such as no sugar added applesauce.
Sugar in canned or frozen fruits	Decrease or eliminate sugar when canning or freezing fruits, or buy unsweetened frozen fruit or fruit canned in its own juices, water, or light syrup.

3 Natural Detox Bath Recipes

Nothing is more relaxing than a warm bath. A relaxing warm detox bath also helps cleanse the body. These natural recipes are a simple, easy and inexpensive way to boost health. It is important to note that these recipes are meant for educational purposes only, so be sure to discuss with your medical provider before adding anything to your health routine.

CLAY DETOX BATH RECIPE

Ingredients

- ½ cup Bentonite Clay
- ½ cup Epsom Salt
- Any essential oils if desired.

Directions: Dissolve the Epsom salts in a warm/hot bath and add essential oils if desired. For the clay there are two options:

1.Vigorously mix the clay into a small amount of water until the clumps are mostly dissolved. Do not use metal for this. Mix with a plastic spoon in a glass jar. Add the clay mix to the bath and soak for at least 20 minutes.

2.Mix that clay with a small amount of water to make a paste. Stand in the tub full of water and rub the clay mix all over your body to create a skin mask and let dry for 5 minutes before sitting down.This provides direct contact with the skin and effectively pulls toxins from the skin. Soak in bath at least 20 minutes or as long as desired. While soaking, use a wash cloth to scrub any remaining clay off the skin.

This bath is great for removing a lot of toxins as the clay binds to heavy metals and the Epsom salt helps pull a variety of toxins from the body while replenishing magnesium levels.

OXYGEN DETOX BATH RECIPE

Ingredients

- 2 cups or more of Hydrogen Peroxide
- 1 tablespoon Dried Ginger Powder

Directions: Fill the tub with warm/hot water and add the hydrogen peroxide and dried ginger. Soak in tub for 30 minutes or as long as desired. This bath is especially helpful during illness as the ginger helps clear congestion and alleviates body aches. It can also be helpful for allergies or skin irritation.

SALT DETOX BATH RECIPE

Ingredients

- 1/4 cup Sea Salt or Himalayan Salt
- 1/4 cup Epsom Salt
- 1/4 cup Baking Soda
- 1/3 cup Apple Cider Vinegar
- Add favorite essential oil if desired (10 drops or so of peppermint, lavender, eucalyptus, etc.)

Directions: Dissolve sea salt or Himalayan salt, Epsom salt, and baking soda in boiling water in a quarter size jar and set aside. Fill tub with warm/hot water and add apple cider vinegar. Pour salt mixture in and add essential oils if using. Soak in bath for 15-20 minutes.

12 Ways to Keep Lymphatic System Flowing Smoothly

1.) Dry body brushing-Using a dry body brush will increase circulation and boost a sluggish lymph system. Start at your arms and legs and use long strokes to move the brush towards your heart. Aim for about five minutes of brushing before you jump in the shower in the morning.

2.) Rebounding- Bouncing on a rebounder or trampoline is the most efficient way to move lymph fluid. Bouncing, a vertical motion exercise smoothly opens and closes the one-way valves that make up the lymphatic system. Jumping on a rebounder, even gently, increases lymph flow by as much as 15-30 times.

3.) Gentle massage- Massage stimulates the lymph nodes and helps promote fluid movement in lymph vessels. Lymph drainage massage is especially supportive of the lymphatic system. Studies show that a gentle massage can push up to 78 percent of stagnant lymph back into circulation. A massage frees trapped toxins. You can also try a lymph drainage massage. It is a special form of massage that specifically targets lymph flow in the body. Whatever type of massage you choose, make sure it is gentle. Too much pressure may feel good on the muscles, but it doesn't have the same lymph-stimulating effects.

4.) Deep breathing- Deep breathing promotes the movement of fluid through the lymphatic system while providing it with fresh oxygen.

5.) Eat a clean diet- Foods that promote a healthy lymph system include organic fruits and veggies, especially leafy greens for their chlorophyll content. Fruits and vegetables supply the lymphatic system with important vitamins, minerals, antioxidants, and phytonutrients. Essential fatty acids in the form of flaxseed oil, spirulina, walnuts, almonds and avocados are also necessary for proper lymph function. Preservatives, artificial sweeteners, refined grains, excess sugar, chemicals and processed foods all put a strain on the lymphatic system.

6.) Drink plenty of water-The lymphatic system depends on a constant supply of fluid, so it's important to drink a lot of water to keep it functioning at its best. Purified or filtered is best.

7.) Eat more raw fruit on an empty stomach- The enzymes and acids in fruit are powerful lymph cleansers. Eat them on an empty stomach for best digestion and maximum lymph-cleansing benefits. Most fruits are digested within 30 minutes or so and quickly help you feel better.

8.) Stay away from soda pop, neon-colored sports drinks and fruit "juices" that are more sugar than fruit. These sugar-color- and preservative laden beverages add to the already overburdened workload your lymph system has to handle.

9.) Eat plenty of green vegetables-To get adequate chlorophyll to help purify your blood and lymph.

10.) Eat raw, unsalted nuts and seeds to power up your lymph with adequate fatty acids. Choose from walnuts, almonds, hazelnuts, macadamias, Brazil nuts, flaxseeds, sunflower seeds and pumpkin seeds.

11.) Add some lymph-boosting herbal teas to your day, such as Echinacea, pokeroot, or wild indigo root tea. Always consult an herbalist or natural medicine specialist before combining two or more herbs, or if you're taking medications or suffer from any serious health conditions. Avoid using herbs while pregnant or lactating and avoid long-term use of any herb without first consulting a qualified professional.

12.) Alternate hot and cold showers for several minutes. The heat dilates the blood vessels and the cold causes them to contract. Avoid this type of therapy if you have a heart or blood pressure condition or if you are pregnant.

The Daniel Fast Food List

All fruit: fresh, frozen, dried, juiced or canned.

All vegetables: fresh, frozen, dried, juiced, or canned

All whole grains: amaranth, barley, brown rice, oats, quinoa, millet, and whole wheat

All nuts & seeds: almonds, cashews, macadamia nuts, peanuts, pecans, pine nuts, walnuts, pumpkin seeds, sesame seeds, and sunflower seeds; unsweetened almond milk, nut butters are also included.

All legumes: canned or dried; black beans, black eyed peas, Cannellini beans, garbanzo beans (chickpeas), great northern beans, kidney beans, lentils, pinto beans, and split peas.

All quality oils: avocado, coconut, grape seed, olive, peanut, sesame, and walnut.

Beverages: distilled water, filtered water, and spring water.

Other: unsweetened almond milk, coconut milk, rice milk, herbs, spices, salt, pepper, unsweetened coconut flakes, seasonings, Bragg's Liquid aminos, soy products, and tofu.

Foods to Avoid During Daniel Fast

- All meat and animal products; bacon, beef, buffalo, eggs, fish, lamb, poultry, and pork.

- All dairy products: butter, cheese, cream, milk and yogurt.

- All sweeteners: agave nectar, artificial sweeteners, brown rice syrup, can juice, honey, molasses, raw sugar, syrups and sugar.

- All leavened bread & yeast: baked goods.

- All refined & processed food products: artificial flavorings, food additives, white flour and white rice.

- All deep fried foods: corn chips, French fries, potato chips.

- Beverages: alcohol, carbonated drinks, coffee, energy drinks.

Relaxation Techniques/Exercises

Relaxation exercises can help reduce stress symptoms and assist you with enjoying a better quality of life. Relaxation isn't only about peace of mind or enjoying a hobby, relaxation techniques can also help you cope with everyday stress. Learning basic relaxation techniques is easy. They involve refocusing your attention on something calming and increasing awareness of your body. It doesn't matter which relaxation technique you choose. What matters is that you try to practice relaxation exercises regularly to experience its benefits.

Types of relaxation techniques include:

Autogenic relaxation: Autogenic means something that comes from within you. In this relaxation technique, you use both visual imagery and body awareness to reduce stress.

Repeat words or suggestions in your mind that may help you relax and reduce muscle tension. For example, you may imagine a peaceful setting and then focus on controlled, relaxed breathing, slowing your heart rate, or feeling different physical sensations, such as relaxing each arm or leg one by one.

Progressive muscle relaxation: In this relaxation technique, you focus on slowly tensing and then relaxing each muscle group. In one method of progressive muscle relaxation, you start by tensing and relaxing the muscles in your toes and progressively working your way up to your neck and head. You can also start with your head and neck and work down to your toes. Tense your muscles for about five seconds and then relax for 30 seconds, and repeat.

Visualization: In this relaxation technique, you form mental images to take a visual journey to a peaceful, calming place or situation.

To relax using visualization, try to incorporate as many senses as you can, including smell, sight, sound and touch. For instance, if you imagine relaxing at the ocean, picture the sound of crashing waves and the warmth of the sun on your body.

Close your eyes, sit in a quiet spot, loosen any tight clothing, and concentrate on your breathing. Aim to focus on the present and think positive thoughts.

Relaxation techniques take practice

As you learn relaxation techniques, you can become more aware of muscle tension and other physical sensations of stress. Once you know what the stress response feels like, you can make a conscious effort to practice a relaxation technique the moment you start to feel stress symptoms. Your ability to relax will improve with practice, so be patient with yourself. If one relaxation technique doesn't work for you, try another technique.

Deep Breathing Exercises

Deep breathing exercises not only keep the mind and body functioning at their best, it can also help lower blood pressure, promote a feeling of calmness/relaxation and help us de-stress.

How is it done? Put one hand on your chest and the other on your belly. Breathe in through your nose, slow breaths in and breathe out through your lips [pursed like you are about to whistle]. Take 6 to 10 deep slow breaths per minute for about 10 minutes.

Liver Support Eating Regimen
Do Not Overeat

Foods to Avoid Completely

- Hydrogenated & partially hydrogenated fats (i.e. margarine)
- Deep fried foods
- Preserved meats (i.e. ham & bacon)
- Fatty meats
- Animal skins
- Processed vegetable oils (most salad dressings, use organic)
- Alcohol
- Coffee
- Colas
- Dark teas (green teas are ok)
- Chocolate

Avoid

- Processed foods
- Wheat products
- Refined sugar
- Corn products
- Simple sugars (honey & maple syrup)
- Fast foods

Decrease Intake of

- Meat
- Dairy products
- Saturated fats (i.e. cheese)

Liver Friendly Fats
- Olive oil (extra virgin best)
- Avocados
- Raw & fresh nuts & seeds (avoid peanuts & cashews)
- Flax seed oil
- Fish oil

Beverages
- Plenty of filtered water with lemon or lime
- Fresh vegetable & fruit juices
- Green tea & other herbal teas

Eat Plenty of
- Organic fruits
- Organic vegetables (cooked or raw)
- Free range meats (organic if possible)
- Beans
- Liver friendly starches: brown rice, wild rice, rice crackers, rice pasta, etc.

Powerful Detox Proteins
- Salmon (4-6 oz)
- Mackerel (4-6 oz)
- Herring (4-6 oz)
- Halibut (4-6 oz)
- Free range chicken (2-4 oz)
- Turkey (2-4 oz)
- Free range extra lean beef (2-4 oz)
- Free range eggs (on occasion)

Scriptural Confirmations
& Affirmations

Confessions of Who I Am In Christ

I thank you Lord that these signs follow me because I believe:

- In Your name I cast out devils; and I speak with new tongues.

- If I take up serpents or if I eat or drink any deadly thing, it will not hurt me. I lay hands on the sick and they recover.

- I thank You Lord God that you have revealed to me the truth concerning the enemy that he has come to steal, and to kill, and to destroy; but You are come that I may have life, and that I may have the abundant life.

And it has come to pass that because I hearken diligently to the voice of the Lord my God, I observe and do all His commandments that He will set me high above all nations of the earth.

- And all blessings shall come on me, and overtake me, because I hearken to the voice of the Lord My God.

- I am blessed in the city, and I am blessed in the country.

- My children both spiritual and natural are blessed, anything I sow, anything I grow, and anything I put my hand to do is blessed.

- I am blessed everywhere I go, and in everything I do.

- I thank you Lord that you will cause any enemy that comes against me to be knocked down and defeated before my face: They will come against me one way and then flee before me seven ways.

- I thank you Lord that you command blessings upon my storage, and in all things that I set my hand to do, and you bless me in the land and homes that you have given me.

- You Lord God establish me as a holy people unto yourself because I keep all of the commandments of you the Lord My God, and I walk in all Your appointed ways.

- All people of the earth shall see that I am called by Your name and they shall be afraid to do or say anything against me.

- And you Lord God make me plenteous in goods, in spiritual and natural children, in material possessions, and in blessings that you have promised to give Your children.

- The Lord opens unto me His good treasure, the heaven to give the rain unto my land in season, and to bless all the work of my hand: and I shall lend unto many nations, and I shall not borrow.

- And you Lord make me the head, and not the tail, and I shall be above only, and I shall not be beneath, because I hearken, observe and do the commandments that you have given.

- And I will not go aside from any of the words that you command, not to the right or to the left nor go after other idols to serve and worship them.

Because the Spirit of Him that raised up Jesus from the dead dwells in me, He that raised up Christ from the dead also quickens my mortal body by His Spirit that dwells in me.

I thank you Lord that you have given rest unto me your child, according to all that You have promised. Not one Word of your good promises have failed, which you promised by the hand of Moses Your servant.

I will not worry about anything, but in everything by prayer and supplication with thanksgiving I will let my requests be made known unto you Lord God. And the peace of God, which passes all understanding, will keep my heart and mind through Christ Jesus.

Father God, I will pay attention to your Words, and incline my ear to your sayings.

- I will not let Your Words depart from my eyes; I will keep them in the midst of my heart.
- For Your Words are life unto those that find them, and health to all their flesh.
- Because Your Words are life to me, and health to all of my flesh.
- I will keep my heart with all diligence; for out of it are the issues of life.

For God has not given me the spirit of fear; but the spirit of power, and of love and of a sound mind.

- I will not fear, because You are with me; I will not be dismayed for you are My God;
- You will strengthen me' yes, You will help me; yes, You will uphold me with the right hand of Your righteousness.
- I will hold fast the profession of our faith without wavering; for You are faithful in Your promises;
- I will not cast away my confidence, which has great recompense of reward.
- I thank you Lord Jesus Christ because You are the same yesterday, and today, and forever.
- I say I am strong.

I thank you Lord Your Word says:

"Beloved, if our heart condemns us not, then have we confidence toward God. And whatsoever we ask, we receive of him, because we keep his commandments, and do those things that are pleasing in his sight."

Therefore, my heart doesn't condemn me and I have confidence toward God and whatsoever I ask I receive of You, because I keep Your commandments, and do those things that are pleasing in Your sight.

I thank You Lord that I have overcome the enemy by the blood of the Lamb, and by the Word of my testimony and we love not our lives unto the death.

Scriptures: Mark 16:17-18; John 10:10; Deuteronomy 28:1-14; Romans 8:11; 1 Kings 8:56; Philippians 4:6-7; Proverbs 4:20-23; 2 Timothy 1:7; Isaiah 41:10; Hebrews 10:23; Hebrews 10:35; Hebrews 13:8; Joel 3:10, 1 John 3:21-22; Revelations 12:11

Daily Confessions: Say It Until You See It

I thank you Father that I and my household seek you daily, give to the church and to others as you instruct, we pray and spend time with you always.

I thank you Father that because I believe on, rely, and adhere to the Words of the Lord Jesus Christ I and my household are saved.

I will shout for joy and be glad, I favor God's righteous cause, yes I will say continually, let the Lord be magnified, which hath pleasure in the prosperity of me His servant.

I thank you Lord that I am the rich which rules over the poor, and I am the lender and not the borrower.

I have a bountiful eye and I am blessed because I give of my sustenance to the poor.

The wealth of the sinner is laid up and available to me.

The Spirit of the Lord God is upon me; because the Lord has anointed me to preach good tidings to the meek; He has sent me to bind up the broken hearted, to proclaim liberty to the captives, and the opening of the prison to those that are bound. To proclaim the acceptable year of the Lord, and the day of vengeance of our God, to comfort all that mourn; to appoint to them that mourn in Zion, to give to them beauty for ashes, the oil of joy for mourning, the garment of praise for the spirit of heaviness, that they might be called trees of righteousness, the planting of the Lord, that He might be glorified.

I thank you Lord that Your Spirit rests upon me, the spirit of wisdom, and understanding, the spirit of counsel and might, the spirit of knowledge and of the fear of the Lord. You have made me to have quick understanding in the fear of the Lord; and I will not judge after the sight of my eyes, nor reprove after the hearing of my ears, but I will judge and reprove only according to what the Spirit of the Lord says.

I thank you Lord that I do all things decently and in order.

When I sit to eat I make conscious and deliberate decisions regarding what I put in this body, I have control over my appetite and I eat only those things which are necessary for the fueling of it to accomplish God's will for my life here on earth. I do not desire dainties or sweets (white or brown sugar) because they are deceitful and do damage to my body without my realizing it.

I thank you Lord that You have given me the tongue of the learned (knowledge, wisdom, and insight) and I know how to speak a Word in season at the right time and right place to all those that are weary.

My mouth, my words

· I will speak of excellent things, and the opening of my lips shall be right things.
· My mouth shall speak truth.
· All the words of my mouth are in righteousness, there is nothing willful, or unfavorable, or obstinately disobedient in them.
· My speech will always be with grace, seasoned with salt.
· My mouth is a well of life.
· Wisdom is found in my lips.
· My tongue is as choice silver.
· My lips feed many.
· My mouth brings forth wisdom.
· My lips know and speak what is acceptable
· My tongue speaks health.

I shall worship the Lord my God and He will bless my bread and my water and He will take sickness away from among me and my loved ones.

Father in the name of Jesus, I thank You that you give me knowledge and skill in all learning and wisdom, and I have understanding in all visions and dreams.

I thank You Father that in all matters of wisdom and understanding I am 10x better than all others who don't know and reverence all mighty God.

Blessed be the name of God forever and ever, for wisdom and might are Yours, and You change the times and the seasons, You remove leaders and set up leaders. You give wisdom to the wise and knowledge to them that have understanding. You reveal the deep and secret things. You know what is in the darkness and the light dwells with You.

I thank You and Praise You, Oh God who has given me wisdom and might and has made known to me what I have asked of You, for You have now revealed this secret thing to me.

I thank You Father for an excellent spirit and knowledge and understanding, interpreting of dreams and showing of hard sentences and dissolving of doubts.

I thank You Lord that light and understanding and excellent wisdom is found in me because Your Spirit dwells within me.

I thank You Father that You give me favor and I am preferred over others; and You have put within me the ability to do all things in excellence and I am promoted in every area of my life.

I thank You Lord that no one can find error or fault in me and I am faithful to do Your will and bring honor and glory to Your Kingdom.

Thank You Father for giving me the tongue of a disciple of Christ and of one who is taught, that I should know how to speak a Word in season to him who is weary. Thank You for waking me morning by morning for my ears to hear as a disciple as one who is taught.

For the Lord God helps me, therefore have I not been ashamed or confounded. Therefore have I set my face like a flint, and I know that I shall not be put to shame.

I declare: No more money troubles. I am financially free. All yokes are removed and that's past, present, and future. All burdens are lifted and that's past, present, and future. We declare right now that we will walk in financial freedom from this day forth.

I thank You Father, that there are no blemishes in me. I am well favored, skillful in all wisdom, and cunning in knowledge, and understanding science and with ability to stand in a king's palace.

"I Have" Confessions

1. I have been made meet to be partakers of the inheritance of the saints in light.

2. I have been delivered from the power of darkness.

3. I have redemption through the blood of Jesus.

4. I have forgiveness of sins through the blood of Jesus

5. I have been presented holy and blameless and unreprovable in God's sight because of Jesus' shed blood. Because I continue in the faith grounded and settled and not moved away from the hope of the gospel.

6. I have the fear of the Lord therefore I hate evil, pride, arrogance, the evil way and forward mouth.

7. I have understanding and strength.

8. I have put on the new man, which is renewed in knowledge after the image of Him that created Him.

9. I have safety in a multitude of wise counselors.

Healing Confession Scriptures
Say What the Word Says (Confession twice daily)

- Because I diligently hearken to the voice of the Lord my God, I do that which is right in His sight, I give ear to His commandments, and I keep all His statutes, therefore He will put none of the diseases on me which has been brought on the world, for You are the Lord that heals me.

- Lord God you have said to us, that whosoever shall say to any mountain or problem, "Be removed and be cast into the sea, and not doubt in our hearts but believe everything that we say will come to pass and we shall have whatsoever we say." And you have said to us that whatever things we desire when we pray, believe that we receive them, and we shall have them, therefore we receive healing and divine health from you now.

- I serve You, the Lord my God, and You bless my bread, and my water; and You take sickness away from the midst of me.

- I serve You, the Lord my God, and You bless my bread, and my water; and You take sickness away from the midst of me.

- I thank You Lord that you take away all sickness from me, all known and unknown diseases of the world will not come near me, but instead will be put on all those that hate You.

Your Word says, and I believe:

As it is written, I had made thee a father of many nations, before him whom he believed, even God, who quickeneth the dead, and calleth those things which be not as though they were. Who against hope believed in hope, that he might become the father of many nations, according to that which was spoken, so shall thy seed be. And being not weak in faith, he considered not his own body, now dead, when he was about a hundred years old, neither yet the deadness of Sara's womb.

He staggered not at the promise of God through unbelief; but was strong in faith, giving glory to God.

Therefore by this Word I believe that I am healed and walk in divine health and I call those things that be not as though they were.

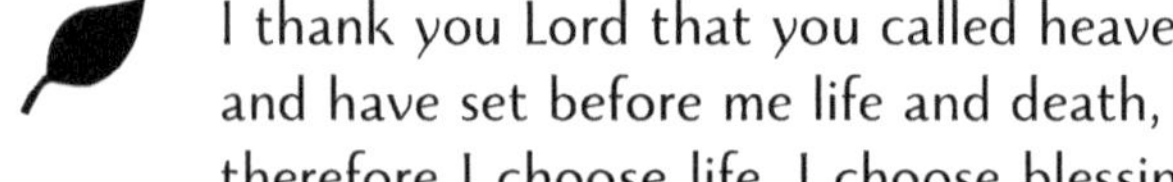

I thank you Lord that you called heaven to record long ago and have set before me life and death, blessing and cursing; therefore I choose life, I choose blessings and both me and my seeds shall live.

So that I may love the Lord my God, and that I will obey His voice, and that I may cleave unto Him, for He is my life, and the length of my days; that I may dwell in the land which he has sworn to my spiritual fathers that He would give me.

I thank you Lord that you have promised to satisfy me with long life, and show me Your salvation.

So that the blessings of Abraham shall come on the Gentiles through Jesus Christ; that we might receive the promise of the Spirit through faith.

I thank you Lord that you forgive all my iniquities; and You heal all my diseases.

I thank you Lord that You have sent Your Word and healed me, and delivered me from all destruction.

Surely You have borne our griefs, and carried our sorrows; yet we did esteem You stricken, smitten of God, and afflicted.

But You were wounded for our transgressions, You were bruised for our iniquities; the chastisement of our peace was upon You and with Your stripes I am healed.

Then said the Lord to me, you have well seen; for I will hasten My Word to perform it.

I thank you Lord that you restore health unto me, and You heal me of my wounds because I have been called an outcast saying, this is Zion whom no man seeks after.

I thank You Lord that Your Word says: Is any sick among you? Let him call for the elders of the church; and let them pray over him, anointing him with oil in the name of the Lord; and the prayer of faith shall save the sick, and the Lord shall raise me up, and any sins that I have committed have been forgiven.

I thank you Lord that I am healed and affliction shall not rise up the second time.

I thank You Lord that you yourself bore my sins in Your own body on the tree that I, being dead to sins, should live unto righteousness; by Your stripes I am healed.

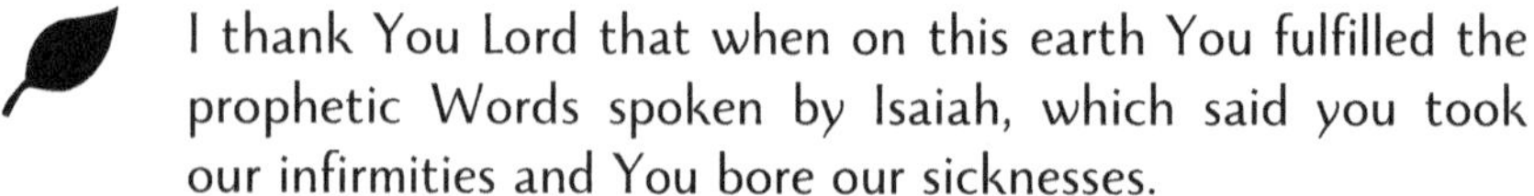 I thank You Lord that when on this earth You fulfilled the prophetic Words spoken by Isaiah, which said you took our infirmities and You bore our sicknesses.

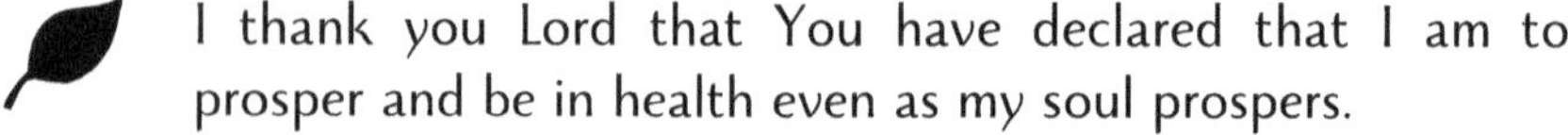 I thank you Lord that You have declared that I am to prosper and be in health even as my soul prospers.

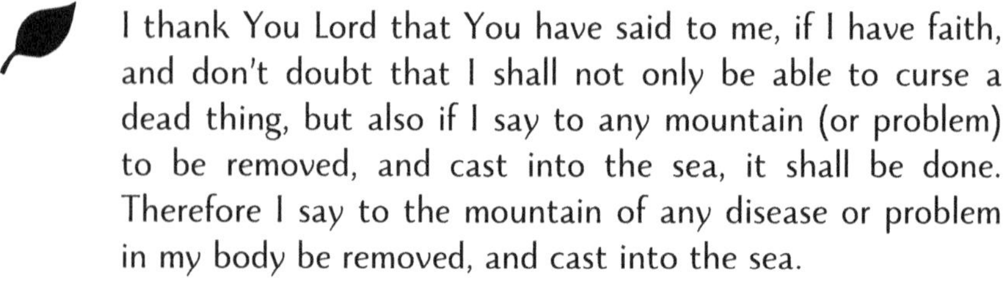 I thank You Lord that You have said to me, if I have faith, and don't doubt that I shall not only be able to curse a dead thing, but also if I say to any mountain (or problem) to be removed, and cast into the sea, it shall be done. Therefore I say to the mountain of any disease or problem in my body be removed, and cast into the sea.

Scriptures: Exodus 15:26; Mark 11:23-24; Exodus 23:25; Deuteronomy 7:15; Romans 4:17-20; Deuteronomy 30:19-20; Psalm 91:16; Galatians 3:13-14; Psalm 103:3; Psalm 107;20; Psalm 118:17; Isaiah 53:4-5; Jeremiah 1:12; Jeremiah 30:17; James 5:14-15; Nahum 1:9; I Peter 2:24; Matthew 8:2-3; Matthew 8:17; 3 John 2; Matthew 21:21.

TCT Kingdom Prayer Affirmation

I loose God's will in my life, His blessings of prosperity, deliverance, healing and salvation IN THE NAME OF JESUS. The Spirit of prophecy rests upon me and those things that I declare shall be established. My steps are ordered of the Lord. The Holy Spirit leads me into all truth. I discern between the righteous and the wicked, between those that serve God and those that don't.

I take authority over this day, IN JESUS NAME that it be prosperous for my spirit, soul, body, and finances. I know my life is covered in the blood. Let me walk in your love and show forth your glory. I thank you Lord that I have a God kind of faith, ever increasing, limitless faith.

I pray for the ministry you have called me to be a part of, for the ministry you have called me to walk in. I thank you for the financial support to do the work unhindered by lack. I thank you for helpers to assist in the work; and for intercessors to hold the ministry up in prayer at all times. I pray that all involved are perfectly united in our common goal, understanding, opinions, and judgments. We stand firmly united in spirit and purpose, working side by side, centering in on the gospel work. We live in harmony and unity, sharing the same love. We do nothing in strife or vain glory. We follow after righteousness, godliness, faith, love, patience, meekness and long-suffering.

TCT Kingdom Prayer Affirmation (cont'd)

I confess that I am called, anointed and equipped to accomplish all God has called me to do. I overcome by THE BLOOD OF THE LAMB and the word of my testimony. I ask you Lord to dispatch ministering angels to their assigned tasks to protect and assist me this day according to Your will and their assignments by your Word. I rebuke any negative expectations. I forgive all people. I receive from the Lord. He is my provider. I thank you for divine appointments with open doors of opportunity. I call forth God ordained increase and multiplication of souls, ministry recruits, and positions. I declare it so, IN JESUS NAME. May the Lord perfect all that concerns me. I stand in the victory Jesus Christ has won for me. AMEN.

Weight/Appetite Control Scriptures

Bind: desire indulgence and gluttony
Loose: self-discipline, will power, and temperance

Thank and praise God daily for the overcoming power of the Word of God.

Mark 8:34, "And when he had called the people unto him with his disciples also, he said unto them, Whosoever will come after me, let him deny himself, and take up his cross, and follow me."

Proverbs 13:25, "The righteous eateth to the satisfying of his soul: but the belly of the wicked shall want."

James 5:16, "Confess your faults one to another, and pray one for another, that ye may be healed. The effectual fervent prayer of a righteous man availeth much."

Luke 21:34, "And take heed to yourselves, lest at any time your hearts be overcharged with surfeiting, and drunkenness, and cares of this life, and so that day come upon you unawares."

Psalm 34:10 "The young lions do lack, and suffer hunger: but they that seek the LORD shall not want any good thing."

Psalm 42:11, "Why art thou cast down, O my soul? and why art thou disquieted within me? hope thou in God: for I shall yet praise him, who is the health of my countenance, and my God."

Psalm 55:18, "He hath delivered my soul in peace from the battle that was against me: for there were many with me."

Psalms 97:10, "Ye that love the LORD, hate evil: he preserveth the souls of his saints; he delivereth them out of the hand of the wicked."

Psalms 103:5, "Who satisfieth thy mouth with good things; so that thy youth is renewed like the eagles."

Psalms 145:18, "The LORD is nigh unto all them that call upon him, to all that call upon him in truth."

Proverbs 10:11, "The mouth of a righteous man is a well of life: but violence covereth the mouth of the wicked."

Proverbs 18:20, "A man's belly shall be satisfied with the fruit of his mouth; and with the increase of his lips shall he be filled."

Proverbs 23:1-5, "When thou sittest to eat with a ruler, consider diligently what is before thee: And put a knife to thy throat, if thou be a man given to appetite. Be not desirous of his dainties: for they are deceitful meat. Labor not to be rich: cease from thine own wisdom. Wilt thou set thine eyes upon that which is not? for riches certainly make themselves wings; they fly away as an eagle toward heaven."

Proverbs 25:27-28, "It is not good to eat much honey: so for men to search their own glory is not glory. He that hath no rule over his own spirit is like a city that is broken down, and without walls."

Proverbs 26:1, "As snow in summer, and as rain in harvest, so honour is not seemly for a fool."

Proverbs 30:8, "Remove far from me vanity and lies: give me neither poverty nor riches; feed me with food convenient for me."

Isaiah 26:3, "Thou wilt keep him in perfect peace, whose mind is stayed on thee: because he trusteth in thee."

Isaiah 40:29, "He giveth power to the faint; and to them that have no might he increaseth strength."

Philippians 4:7, "And the peace of God, which passeth all understanding, shall keep your hearts and minds through Christ Jesus."

Hebrews 10:35, "Cast not away therefore your confidence, which hath great recompence of reward."

Notes

INTRODUCTION

American Tract Society Bible Dictionary, Retrieved from www.studylight.org.

Eason's 1897 Bible Dictionary, Retrieved from www.studylight.org

Unless otherwise noted all scripture quotations are from the King James Version of the Bible.

MODULE 1

N. Barnard, MD, *Breaking the Food Seduction* (New York: Martin Press, 2003).

S. Horne, *Body Systems Questionnaire*, 2017, retrieved from www.treelite.com.

MODULE 2

S. Burroughs, *The Master Cleanse*, n.d., retrieved from www.circle-of-life.net.

D. Colbert, MD, *Toxic Relief* (Lake Mary: Siloam Press, 2001).

A. Grittleman, A., *Sugar: Toxic Invader#1*, n.d., retrieved from www.shareguide.com.

Heal Your Body With Food,2008, retrieved from www.coreperformance.com.

M. Pick, NP, *Detoxification-Imbalance and Your Weight*, n.d., retrieved from www.marcellepick.com.

M. Pick, NP, *Detoxification-It's More Than A Week Long Cleanse*, n.d., retrieved from www.marcellepick.com.

Completely Rebuild Your Body From the Inside Out, n.d., retrieved from www.undergroundreporter.com.

D. Colbert, MD, *Walking in Divine Health (Lake Mary: Siloam Press,* 1999).

Healthy Eating: Make it Happen, retrieved from www.eatright.org.

M. Pick, NP, *Essential Nutrition for Healthy Weight*, n.d., retrieved from www.marcellepick.com.

J.J. Smith, *10 Day Green Smoothie Cleanse* (New York: Atria Paperback, 2014).

MODULE 3

N. Barnard, MD, *Breaking the Food Seduction* (New York: St. Martin Press, 2003).

MODULE 4

D.Colbert,MD, *Toxic Relief (*Lake Mary:Siloam Press, 2001).

B. Pilon, *10 Benefits of Fasting That Will Surprise You*, retrieved from www.lifehack.org.

J. Shakeshaft, *6 Breathing Exercises to Relax in 10 Minutes*, 2012, " retrieved from www.healthland.com.

MODULE 5

Fitness: Walking For Wellness, retrieved from www.webmd.com.

MODULE 6

N. Barnard, MD, *Breaking the Food Seduction* (New York: St. Martin Press, 2003).

D. Colbert, MD, *Walking in Divine Health* (Lake Mary: Siloam Press, 1999).

APPENDIX

D. Vanadia, *Stop Being Sweet*, retrieved from www.vanadia.com/stopbeingsweet/quiz/

B. Kim, ND, *Apple Cleanse*, 2016, retrieved from www.drbenkim.com.

Lyzabeth Lopez, *Do You Need the Cleanse Quiz*, retrieved from www.trainwithlyzabeth.com/detox-cleanse-quiz/

N. Barnard, MD, Breaking the Food Seduction (New York: St. Martin Press, 2003).

D. Colbert, MD, Walking In Divine Health (Lake Mary: Siloam Press, 1999).

J. Newman-Davis, *Scripture Keys For Kingdom Living* (Denver: Scripture Keys Ministries).

M. Schoffro-Cook, *11 Ways to Boost Your Lymphatic System for Great Health,* retrieved from www.care2.com.